Introduction by W. Terrence Gordon

Though it focuses mainly on the effects of printing, this essay from *Printing Progress* (1959), pages 89-112, anticipates themes from McLuhan's *Gutenberg Galaxy* and *Understanding Media*. Thus, "the printed word is an arrested moment of mental activity" brackets a medium and the "pure process" of thought exempt from the typical action of media in pairs, as elaborated in *Understanding Media*. A similar comment reveals the extent to which McLuhan is both analyst and historian of media: "[P]rinting was not an accident but the focal point of a great cluster of technological skills, each of which had a long social history." References to the Gutenberg era are, of course, frequent and explicit: "For some years now I have been concerned with the Gutenberg era as a period in which the vitality of new forms spread into all phases of life and consciousness." It is also clear that McLuhan is moving inexorably toward the formulation of his laws of media: "From one point of view the scanning finger of the TV screen is at once the transcending mechanism and a throwback to the world of the scribe. Any history of technology is filled with such unexpected reversals of form resulting from new advances." In borrowing from linguistics to develop his laws of media, McLuhan also suggests an agenda for linguists: "To detail the effects of phonetic linguistic culture on earlier language structure would be a worthy task." More central to McLuhan's own program and to the mindset he wishes to engender, in order to launch the educational reform required by the post-Gutenberg era, is a radical commitment to cast off the shackles of *visual* orientation and embrace "the *visionary* quality of scientific discovery" (my emphasis). — WTG

Printing and Social Change

The present is a fruitful point at which to begin to look at the changes brought about by print. After five centuries of print we are surrounded by forms for transmitting information, many of which seem to have little to do with print. So it is this very challenge and rivalry to the printed forms of communication which have made possible a more careful inquiry into the nature and effects of the word in printed form. When, however, the views of the past five hundred years on this subject are consulted there appears a notable absence of awareness of any profound influence from print. For the first century and more the printed word was seen as a more convenient form of the manuscript page, much as it was once fashionable to speak of the newspaper as the popular book, of the automobile as the horseless carriage, the radio as wireless, tv as a sort of movie-in-the-home.

Rudolph Arnheim's observation concerning the early stages of film is relevant here. It occurs in his excellent Film as Art: [1]

> The history of human ingenuity shows that almost every innovation goes through a preliminary phase in which the solution is obtained by the old method, modified or amplified by some new feature.

The earlier images of any process seem to have a tendency to obscure the immediately present phase by creating an unreal view, so that what was felt and what was actually assimilated at the time, are quite different sets of facts. In the case of print, so striking, indeed, is the discrepancy between what was thought to be happening and what can now be seen to have occurred, that it is helpful to ask whether there is not some quality in the very character of the printed word which diverts attention from its power to impose its own assumptions, or to set into operation a whole chain of personal and social consequences.

Having asked myself this question some time ago, the following feature emerged: the printed word is an arrested moment of mental movement. To read print is to act both as movie projector and audience for a mental movie. The reader attains a strong feeling of participation in the total motions of a mind in the process of thinking. But is it not basically the printed word's 'still shot' that fosters a habit of mind which tackles all problems of movement and change in terms of the unmoved segment or section?

---

1 University of California Press, Berkeley, 1957, p. 174

Has not print inspired a hundred different mathematical and analytical procedures for explaining and controlling change in terms of the unchanging? Have we not tended to apply this very static feature to print itself and talked only of its quantitative effects? Do we not speak more of the power of print to increase knowledge and to extend literacy than the most obvious features of song, dance, painting, perception, poetry, architecture, and town planning?

Today we are aware that any pattern of knowledge or of perception is affected by new information and by other co-existing patterns. We are now in the age of the live or the dynamic model and of the *field theory* in physics and of *game theory* in economics in terms of which the most rapidly shifting changes of structure can be felt and discerned. [2] But in moving into the electronic age where all is simultaneous, we also become more sensitive to the values and unused possibilities of print.

For some years now I have been concerned with the Gutenberg era as a period in which the vitality of new forms spread into all phases of life and consciousness. Today, many people express concern lest the rival electronic forms for handling information should destroy the values and achievements of the printed forms. Since the telegraph, however, we have been launched into the present electronic age, and the craft and uses of print have steadily increased. But even if such were not the case there could be nothing to fear in looking as directly as possible at the drama of events before and since Gutenberg, for it is a continuing drama, the earlier events of which are as relevant now as the opening motifs of a musical work are to its later effects.

---

2 See *Strategy in Poker, Business and War* by John MacDonald, W. W. Norton and Co. New York, 1950

Others have noted how the technology of printing from movable type resembles more recent assembly-line production. Closer inspection suggests that there is nothing accidental in the resemblance. Industrialization depends on habits of analysis of process and movement which are in the very matrix of print both as production and as consumption. Printing would appear to be entitled to the claim of being the first mechanization of a complex handicraft. And printing was not an accident but the focal point of a great cluster of technological skills, each of which had a long social history. The five hundred years since print began have been years of the extension of mechanization to many handicrafts besides that of the scribe. Sigfried Giedion's *Mechanization Takes Command* [3] is a recent account of this process.

From one point of view the scanning finger of the TV screen is at once the transcending of mechanism and a throwback to the world of the scribe. Any history of technology is filled with such unexpected reversals of form resulting from new advances. Let us consider a few points about the pre-Gutenberg world of the scribe and the manuscript. The achievement of the phonetic alphabet was a late phase of scribal culture and remains an achievement embodied within Western printing. The peculiarity of the phonetic alphabet is that meaning is divorced from the sound of the letters. The letters are the visual equivalents of a limited number of sounds, but the visual forms have no complex semantic structure such as naturally accrues in syllables and words in their daily uses. This clean sweep of meaning by technical abstraction may have some correspondence with the new mathematics of our time which provide an unencumbered instrument for considering relationships which could not be managed in the

---

3 Oxford University Press, New York, 1948

more complex social medium of speech. Writing, as such, is the translation of the audible into the visible, and phonetic writing permits the translation of any spoken language into one and the same visual forms. Thus, the possessors of phonetic writing had an instrument of cultural penetration and assimilation previously unknown. May not the history of the Western world's conquest of many cultures be explicable from this point of view? For technology, as Lymon Bryson said, is explicitness, [4] and the phonetic form enables the user to make any tongue visually explicit. Is not the Gutenberg revolution itself a further stage of explicitness in the management of complex experience?

The effects of phonetic writing in the Graeco-Roman world are co-extensive with that period of civilization. H. A. Innis in his *Empire and Communications* [5] has given us a pioneer study on this subject which, though not definitive, is most helpful. Papyrus as a writing surface especially offered a cheap, light material which permitted the control of armies and empires over wide areas. The same accessible material when used with phonetic writing encouraged extensive literacy, and literacy made possible the systematic sub-division and analysis of knowledge and experience. Thus, our own division of the arts and sciences, as well as the basic postulates and procedures within them, occurred quite speedily after the achievement of phonetic writing. In oral or pre-literate societies, on the other hand, knowledge is less specialized and more commonly shared by all of the group. Writing brings not only specialized knowledge but individualism as a social possibility and preference, marking the basic difference between the tribal and the civilized man, and the very concept of the citizen. For the *civis* [6] is the product of written legal codes administered by literate communities.

---

4 *The Next America*, Harper and Bros. New York, 1952, p. 41

5 Oxford Clarendon Press, London, 1950

6 The *civis*, or citizen, was a city man as opposed to the tribal, oral man

The literate man is one who is accustomed to the inner translation of sight into sound and of sound into sight, a complex activity for which he pays by psychic withdrawal, a weakening of sensuous life and a considerable lessening of the power of recall. But in return he obtains analytic mastery of specific areas of knowledge, and especially the power of *applied* science for social purposes. The increase of inner self-awareness resulting from the incessant translation of sound into sight and sight into sound also enhances his sense of individual identity and fosters that inner dialogue or conscience within, which we rightly associate with the very citadel of civilized awareness.

To detail the effects of phonetic linguistic culture on earlier language structure would be a worthy task. Mere hints must suffice here. Writing streamlines the vast gothic sound structures of oral peoples, reducing both inflectional and syntactical forms to much simpler conditions. That process continues today to the consternation of many for whom headlines like

HIX NIX STIX PIX
or
BERRA'S BIG BAT BANISHES BUMS

appear as a savage recurrence. In fact it is the primitive man who employs the most complex and precise modes of language, and it is the civilized man who is always seeking the simplest forms.

Educationally, writing made as much difference to society as printing did to the older educational methods and aims. Basically the manuscript forms of codified knowledge, whether in fifth-century Athens or in twelfth-century Paris, had similar patterns. H. J. Chaytor's *From Script to Print* [7] is invaluable to anybody who wants to learn what the manuscript meant to poetry. What it meant to education before printing remains unstudied, though some aspects are fairly clear. For example, the reading of manuscripts aloud was no mere whim. The sheer slowness of such reading elicits the strategy of mumble as an aid to decipherment. Parchment and vellum were so costly that the scribes resorted to many means of abbreviation which made reading aloud almost necessary. The newspapers of today resort to their own abbreviations to a degree which will make them difficult for readers in a decade or so, unless the readers be supplied with manuals and guides to our system. One need go no further than the CIO, AF of L, NRA, WPA, NATO, UNESCO variety of abbreviation, plus the entire range of those in commerce and sports, radio stations and airlines. But the entire genre is post-telegraph. Perhaps even now few people know what the letters stand for. But slow reading in the ancient and medieval world imposed also the validity of memorization, since it was not practicable to use manuscripts as paginated works of handy reference. It was quicker to memorize than to refer to a text. Moreover, the West before printing was still an oral society in some degree and took for granted a degree of memory achievement which would stagger us now. Hand in hand with memorized reading went the habit of rapid oral exchange of knowledge so acquired. Thus, the medieval school and university were places of recitation and disputation with texts being heard verbatim and being commented on at high speed. The medieval schoolboy had first to make his own texts, grammar and commonplace books. He did not, however, make a dictionary because the idea of words as having fixed alphabetized meanings would have been unthinkable before printing.

---

7 Heffer and Sons, Cambridge, 1945

One basic feature of manuscript culture which can easily be overlooked is its requirement of intense meditation on individual words. This leads in one direction to etymological effort, and in the other to minute philosophical definition — sidore of Seville's *Etymologiœ*, on one hand; Scotus Erigena, on the other. Both of these divergent stresses were found in the ancient world as well, but they are much less a feature of the Gutenberg era. In short, many of the characteristic aims and procedures of the medieval world which the Renaissance humanists found distasteful are those of a society dependent for teaching and study on manuscripts and the spoken word. The image of ancient Greece and Rome that the Renaissance humanists formed from the printed word was much distorted by the medium of print and by their antipathy for the monks and schoolmen whose conditions of culture were actually closer in many ways to Greece and Rome than those conditions which came in with printing.

At the same time that Gutenberg's Bible appeared in Germany there was a great fad in Italy associated with the *camera obscura*. It was found to be possible to sit in a darkened room and by means of a pinhole on one side of the room to see on the opposite side the landscape and moving figures from the outside world reflected on the inner wall. Leonardo da Vinci describes the discovery in his notes. Interest increased and a lens was substituted for the pinhole. Then the lens was put in a box and the upside-down imagery was corrected by mirrors. As Erik Barnouw comments in his *Mass Communication*: [8]

> The box, still thought of as a small room, was called a dark room or 'camera obscura.' This camera could be aimed at a landscape, street, garden

8 Rinehart + co., New York, 1956, p.14

> party. A group of people looking in amazement at the moving images in the box may well have resembled a group watching television ... By the 1600's, painters in many countries were using it to solve problems of perspective ... The next step was obvious. Could the image be preserved, saving the artist even more work?

In a word, but for chemistry the West then stood on the movie threshold.

My own suggestion is that the printed word stands at the beginning of that process of development of which the movie is both an ultimate stage and also a reversal of the characteristics of the original stage. As William Ivins analysed it in *Prints and Visual Communication*,[9] the woodcut and engraving moved through many stages of statement about the visible world, achieving an ever more subtle syntax, until photography suddenly presented us with total statement minus syntax.

The suggestion that print from movable type created a new kind of codification of reality, a new way of representing and communicating mental activity is readily assented to. But to relate this new form of expression and statement to the science and culture of its time needs the scrutiny and collaboration of many minds. Printing was no solitary invention but rather a cluster of many technological achievements which had accumulated over the centuries. From the twelfth century the manufacture of paper had made possible a great increase in manuscript books which promoted concentration on the problems of book production. The same increase had fostered the habits of mind of the reader of books which received such sudden extension after Gutenberg. One of those habits is precisely the awareness of perspective as it

---

9 Cambridge, Harvard University Press, 1953, p. 128

was called by painters — the fixed point of view of the artificially arrested gaze. Such is the stance of the private student closeted with an author.

No less impressive than the new fact of perspective in painting and history was the great change in the subject matter of painting after Giotto (1267-1337). Gilson in his *Painting and Reality* [10] sees that painting until Cézanne (1839-1906) became a means of providing information about the external world. Before Giotto a painting had been a thing. With Cézanne a painting again became a thing in its own right and not a means of presenting or describing the outer world. The representational and the realistic as central aim in painting and poetry is, however complexly, related to the new habits of a reading public. It is my suggestion that reading involves an analytic habit of awareness that provides experience with the static individualistic perspective. We have long spoken of the rise of historical perspective in the Renaissance. The medieval historical sense was almost timeless because it lacked the dimension of a vanishing point provided by static visual perspective. Before printing nobody had time to read around and through an entire period. Men knew some texts, some episodes, some authors. But after printing, a reader could cover authors and periods comprehensively, experiencing his survey as a kind of Tamburlaine conquest of empires. So long as history is read privately the fact of fixed perspective is built into the learning process, a subliminal factor all the more potent for being unconscious. And it is this inherent perspectivism in reading itself, especially the reading of print, that may well have communicated its pattern to painting and other arts.

10 Pantheon Books, New York, 1957, pp. 284-285

In tracing the social consequences of printing it is difficult to select evidence that is separate from a great range of related matters. For example, print quickly transformed the vernacular tongues into new media of instruction which soon supplanted Latin. Latin had been for centuries the main channel of literacy and of articulate thought, but when classical Latin could be seen by all, it was felt to be inexpedient to speak Latin any more. Latin was dropped in its spoken form in order that it might be written in its classical form. Spoken Latin was felt to be barbarous and inept as soon as print had familiarized the literate world with Cicero. This is familiar knowledge today, but it has never been related to the effects of printing. However, C. S. Lewis in his *English Literature in the Sixteenth Century* [11] blasts the humanists for their attitudes to both spoken and written Latin, adopting the strong oral bias of the twentieth century. Lewis, in fact, is as indifferent to the causes which led the humanists into their position against spoken Latin as he is to the new causes today which again give us sympathy with the oral tradition and the spoken word in all its forms. The temptation is to fall into the habit of moral evaluation and indictment and to ignore the circumstances which shape our modes of perception and judgment. This is not to advocate relativism but merely to suggest that we give due regard to our daily experience that circumstances alter cases. Print was a complex new situation which altered and continues to alter many cases.

Writing his *Utopia* in 1512, St. Thomas More spoke of the revolution in the world of learning in his time as follows:

> Your scholastic philosophy is not unpleasant among friends in familiar communication, but in the councils of Kings, where great matters be debated

---

11 Oxford University Press, London, 1953.

> and reasoned with great authority these things have no place . . . [for] speculative philosophy thinks all things suitable for all occasions. There is another philosophy that is more urbane, that knows as you would say her own stage, and therefore orders and behaves herself in the play that she has in hand, playing her part with comeliness, uttering nothing out of due order and fashion.

This brief passage is packed with implications, some of which are relevant to be considered here. That scholastic philosophy is '*not unpleasant among friends*' points accurately to its person-to-person oral character, a basic aspect of it which has long been obscured by meeting it only in printed form. Moreover, this intimate oral type of discourse '*thinks all things suitable for all occasions.*' Speedy oral processing of problems permits that they be tackled from many directions simultaneously, in the pattern which James Joyce revived for *Finnegans Wake*: an 'every way roundabout with the intrusions from above and below.' Even the metaphor of the theater which More invokes, calls to mind a similar switch in method in drama, for the medieval stage had been cyclic and simultaneous in presenting many scenes and episodes at once like a three-ring circus. Whereas the new humanist theater developed the proscenium arch with its single perspective such as a single page presents to a reader. Concern for the dramatic unities naturally emerges with the proscenium arch. It is a major difference between the styles of Dante and Milton.

It is all very well, says More, for free-wheeling speculators to swarm all over an area of thought, '*but in the councils of Kings, where great matters be debated,*' the steady pursuit of one matter at a time is necessary. One main key to the contribution of print to the world of thought and action is that the theme of 'one thing at a time' does not strike us as a novel discovery nor as a deep necessity. It never occurred to the oral scholastic world as a desirable aim. But in 1512 when the presses were new the idea of lineal processing of problems seemed the exciting and revolutionary method which it was. The chain of efficient causation, the chain of being, the chain of association became the preoccupations of the next centuries. But when More wrote his *Utopia* the oral schoolmen were still in control of philosophy and theology and of higher education. Their formidably precise chatter about all problems was the intellectual currency. But the new problems resulting from the new technology of the age banished them from the scene in a short space for the very reasons which More mentions. The world was filling up with new power derived from new technology. The new commerce as much as the new learning depended on the existence of many literate laymen for whom the new media of the vernaculars, as well as the new medium of print, were not just channels of information but new modes of experience. And print it was with its portentous rows of cast metal which provided the mental rails for the swift developments of the Renaissance. Print provided not only the transportation but patterns for thoughts. The Renaissance turned to the conquest of method.

More's passage contains also this import, that the speaker '*in the councils of Kings*' cannot afford to be scientifically objective in the pursuit of the many facets of truth. The sense in which, in these councils, '*great matters be debated and reasoned with great authority*' is not so much the authority of reason as of personal and national power and prestige. The imponderables weighed in such discussion are the consequences of action directed among infinite variables of personal choice and collective whim. And for such discussion it is not the training of the logician but the rhetorician that is decisive.

Print made possible the extensive restoration of the classical program of encyclopedism in the arts and sciences, as well as oratorical presentation. So far as the humanist program is concerned, Cicero's *De Oratore* is the key. It inspired a great adaptation to sixteenth-century conditions in Castiglione's *Courtier.* [12] But Erasmus, the friend of More, was equally influential in sponsoring the Roman ideal of eloquent wisdom achieved by sheer verbal mastery. The program soon became the basis of English gentlemanly or governing class education and so remained till almost the present day.

In this same passage from the *Utopia* More shows complete awareness of the changed conditions of inter-personal and international relations which made the old learning irrelevant. He is hardly aware of the extent to which print was not only the cause of the changes but the hope of their effective resolution. That is to say, Erasmus and More were educational reformers. They saw the classroom as the scene of a desirable revolution as much as John Dewey ever did. Whereas Dewey announced that the student must become co-teacher, Erasmus and More saw the printed text book as the appointed means of change. If the printed Bible could become religion without walls, the printed book offered boundless possibilities to the educator. For until the Renaissance, class-room time was spent to a great degree in making rather than in studying the text. The stress which William Ivins has given, in *Prints and Visual Communication*, to the new power of

---

12 The adaptation from the conditions of republican and imperial Rome to the small Renaissance courts meant a new personal and psychological stress.

exactly repeatable information has not yet found its analyst and commentator in terms of the printed word. Such a commentator would be obliged to examine the effects of this exact repeatability in developing a new consumer orientation in market place and study alike. It was the spectre of an entirely consumer-oriented world that inspired the gloomy prose of Ortega y Gassett's *Revolt of the Masses*.

An accessible and familiar instance of the producer-consumer contrast occurs in the prose of Donne and Browne in the seventeenth century. A recent discussion of these great writers by Gilbert Phelps [13] stresses that Donne, who is scholastic and dialectical in his oral intensity and fervor, offers '*continual heat and motion.' Browne, on the other hand, is the complete bookman whose 'curious and roving mind delights in illustrating an argument with all kinds of unexpected references, examples, and allusions-and in embellishing the theme with numerous quotations . . . he speaks as an amateur and a spectator rather than as a participant.*'

Today when we are experiencing anew the pressures and pleasures of active participation roles, it is helpful to understand that even a tendency to oral culture gives a powerful drive towards the fusion of producer-consumer roles, just as the printed word tends to separate these functions and to create specialists on both sides of the gap.

This is not to make value judgments. Donne, the medievalist, is oral, active, aggressive and engages the reader in the same restless role. Browne, the charming humanist, is a master at cultivating the gentle reader, playing up his whimsical personality as

---

13 *From Donne to Marvell*, Hutchinson's University Library, London, 1956, pp. 122-3

a principal component in his entertainment. These are equally legitimate modes of operation but obviously very distinct in their producer-consumer biases.

It is curious that as compared with Europe and England, America's educational establishment has been consumer oriented in arts and letters as well as in science and invention. Only in the past thirty years or so has there been a strong new trend to producer bias in education and the arts. Roger Sessions, the composer, has recently documented this theme in his book, *Reflections on the Music Life in The United States.* [14]

The producer-consumer split in economics, politics and letters was naturally geared to the great mechanical power of the Gutenberg invention. In pre-mechanical economies there is much interfusion of the roles of producer and consumer, and today, the electronic age, which is post-mechanical in a sense, is already trying to become a do-it-yourself age for reasons to be noted later.

It is entirely natural that rulers should look on print as a heaven-sent means of providing their subjects with uniform instructions, counsel and commands. It is equally natural that subjects should look on the book as a great incentive to individual self-rule and general release from social conformity. The antithetic attitudes of publishers and readers have provided several centuries of dramatic clash. But the American colonists in particular represented a group with intense consumer orientation toward print. The readers' freedom to choose what to read, and the freedom of the press to print what it felt the public wanted to read

---

14 Merlin Press, New York, 1956

became the basis of a social experiment geared to the dynamics of printing such as no other society had seen before or since.

It is natural to quail before the problems of discussing the effect of printing on the religious life of the West. Because it is a little-studied subject despite the great importance of the theme, it is easy to provide some striking perspectives. For example, the intense individualism engendered by solitary, silent reading certainly had its counterpart in the claim for private judgment of Scripture. But precisely what the 'literal interpretation' of such private judgment consisted in is not easy to discover. Aquinas had said that the literal interpretation contained all possible meanings at once. But the sixteenth-century Protestants seem to have felt that literal interpretation was whatever appeared plausible during the act of reading. While private reading and interpretation of Scripture fostered a great amount of schism and religious anarchy, print had equally the effect of creating congregational unity such as was unknown to the medieval world. Similarly, print while encouraging intense economic and political individualism created a high degree of national unity. It is not an easy question to explain why print should do this, but the printed word and nationalist fervor go hand-in-hand. Is it that seeing one's mother tongue in splendid technological form creates an image of collective unity? At least in the matter of worship it is plain enough that if all members of the group are supplied with identical hymn books the focus of group unity shifts outward to the service itself.

In his *Liturgical Piety*, [15] Father Louis Bouyer cites a conversation between Cranmer and Gardiner which occurred while both were

---

15 University of Notre Dame Press, Notre Dame, Indiana, 1954, p. 2

still Catholic priests. Cranmer said, *'How sad it is that the people in the nave of the church do not understand anything about what is being celebrated in the sanctuary!'* And Gardiner answered, *'Don't worry about that, it has never occurred to them that they might want to understand it.'* And Father Bouyer adds: *'How distressing it is for us now to consider that it was the future heretic who had the more truly Catholic reaction!'*

In The *Reformation in England*, [16] Father Hughes cited Gardiner on the mode of assisting at Mass in earlier periods:

> And therefore it was never meant that people should indeed hear the Matins or hear the Mass, but be present there and pray themselves in silence . . . And I have known that, after their little devotions were said, as they called them, some used to gather by the penny or two pence such money as they had lent in gross. But as for hearing of Mass in deed, some well occupied, heard not, and some, evil occupied, heard not neither.

Obviously it had not occurred to Gardiner that the clamor to 'hear the Mass' came from the eye on the page, or that the new desire to follow the mass collectively was the result of the individualist book form which had newly begun to reshape human sensibility. And is it not strange that the oral tradition for which Gardiner speaks unwittingly should have made much of private devotions for congregations while the new book-patterned congregations insisted from their newly discovered collective unity on the right of each to be a complete anarchist?

These complex events seem to have a psychodynamic of their own which is related to the new printed forms of experience.

16 Hollis and Carter, London, 1950

Today, for example, literate people don't want to follow just the text of the Mass but want the dialogue Mass. The electronic technology of the West since the telegraph has created a world in which everything happens at once. More, in his *Utopia*, saw that scholasticism was doomed because the new practical world of affairs required minds for which experience could be processed one bit at a time. Today, is not the reverse becoming true? The electronic age finds it both natural and necessary to be aware of every kind of situation from many points of view simultaneously. For perspectivism, we substitute cubism, in which the spectator sees at once from inside and outside, from above and below. This insistence on an inclusive image or consciousness is strikingly at variance with the exclusive and specialist focus of the literary mind in its first phase. This habit of successive analysis, which derives from the power of printed words to impose their form on our mental processes, we call lineal. And this lineality has been the means of creating most of the forms of order in the arts and practical life of the past five centuries. It is the absence of this power to line things up habitually in linked and orderly succession which clearly marks the pre-Gutenberg man and even more the pre-literate man.

In his *Two-Edged Sword*, [17] John L. McKenzie, S. J., shows how biblical studies in the twentieth century have abandoned the concept of the lineal, stenographic structure of Scripture. Since the prophet was the antithesis of the scribe, it is absurd to think of him as waiting for words to be set down in a line. From the scribal point of view it is easy to arrive at the idea of the Bible as a sort of dictionary, or to think of literature as a storehouse of archetypes repeating the patterns of a cosmic cookie-cutter. Without preju-

---

17 Bruce Publishing Co., Milwaukee, 1956

dice to literary qualities, we today can also see that the prophet as inspired instrument was totally so. Not just his pen but his whole being and the culture which nourished it, were the instrument for recording the voice of the Lord:

Modern control and use of natural forces was not known to the Hebrews, nor did the wildest fancy dream of anything like it . . . the ancient Hebrews were prephilosophical; the most ordinary patterns of modern thought were unknown to them. Logic as a form of mental discipline they lacked. Their language is the speech of the simple man who sees motion and action rather than static reality, static reality as concrete rather than abstract.

In a word, the Hebrews were oral people for whom the arrest of mental experience or of the inner word, either by writing or print, was not constitutive of experience. The '*static reality*' of which Father McKenzie speaks is the by-product of writing and printing. Further attributes of the ancient Hebrew are also relevant to an understanding not only of the effects of print on culture but to a recognition of some of our own oral tendencies in the electronic age. Their language

prefers nouns to adjectives or it does not even like to make the obvious distinction between a substance and its properties. It sees reality rather as it is than as it is intellectually apprehended, in its large outlines and in its superficial and tangible qualities. The sentences of the Hebrew are simple statements of subject and predicate, following one another without subordination; the Hebrew looked on all propositions as having much the same weight, and rarely attempted that precise statement of the inter-relation of propositions which is expressed by grammatical subordinations. The language is repetitive, for repetition is almost the only form of argument and emphasis which the Hebrew knew. Johannes Pedersen has said that thinking for the Hebrews was to grasp a totality; for the modern man, thinking is rather an analysis of a totality. [18]

Today our intense interest in totalities and organic unities gives sharp salience to our awareness of what writing and print have done to create systems of value and patterns of experience. Continuing his contrast of the ancient Hebrew and modern man, Father McKenzie says,

> But to the Hebrews, faith in the Lord was never a matter of assimilating a body of truth, but of surrender to a person. Even in such phrases as instruction and the word of the Lord, they had no notion of redeeming the notions from ignorance. Their prophets were not teachers. When Alexander conquered the ancient Semitic world, he saw himself as a missionary carrying Greek civilization . . . into the darkness of the ignorant heathen world, and he succeeded even more than he had dreamed. The Hebrews had nothing of this sort to offer, and not until they came in contact with the Greek world and Greek learning did they begin to think themselves possessed of a message for the mind. [19]

In a word, the Greeks, with their phonetic alphabet and their systematic analysis of arts and sciences based on that alphabet, had an effective technology to offer.

To approach the new forms assumed by the arts after printing is to enter on a tricky terrain. It is easy to explain that in music, for example, repeatable notation meant new possibilities of both vocal and instrumental ensemble or togetherness. The popular madrigal, for example, with its parts for several voices, could never have begun without printed notes and words. But the very precision of choral effects so achieved led swiftly to the substitu-

---

18 loc. cit.

19 loc. cit.

tion of instruments for human voices. Until print, instruments tended to be strictly subordinate to voice and words. Print liberated instruments to discover a life of their own. Sonata and symphony are musical forms entirely dependent on printed scores. But words suffered from the divorce of music and poetry, and the greatest musical bent of our own time has been to restore harmony among the sister arts of music and poetry.

If music gained new life from its independence from poetry, poetry, too, took on very different attributes once it could be read silently or spoken without being sung. This is an unstudied subject, but the Elizabethan drama was a new popular form of poetic speech which was held by the learned in the same low esteem as Hollywood is today. Educated taste could find no language to praise verse not set to music. But then suddenly the erudite John Donne seized upon the language of the popular stage in which to write his witty songs and sonnets. The effect on other poets was very great, and both devotional and profane poetry suddenly appeared in the homely garb of popular verse from the stage. This revolution was not unlike the one undertaken by T. S. Eliot and others in providing poetry today with the rhythms and tones of jazz and the blues, accompanied by a montage of imagery borrowed from the newspaper and the movie.

A change of even greater significance than that effected by print between words and music occurred in the attitude to character in literature. In Chaucer, realism never detracts from a polyphony of character themes. In his time it was natural to accept a character as a melodic theme to be heard simultaneously with others, just as in an oral society many voices speak at once, while in a literate world one voice is at least expected to be heard at a time. Until about 1600 in art, literature, and music, the only known way of organizing a structure was that of the horizontal song technique with its superimposed or parallel themes and melodies. Shakespeare is in most ways related to the older modes of oral tradition in his art. Marlowe, Jonson, Beaumont and Fletcher — all have accepted the new painterly world of flat, analyzed characters in a way Shakespeare never did. When we say, therefore, that Shakespeare draws his people in the round, we are noting the auditory depth with which his music invests the least gesture or intonation of his characters. The complexity of his characters is often the effect of all the other characters being simultaneously present in the auditory space provided by the music of his language.

But this was not the new mode. Shakespeare lacked fashionable newness and smartness in large degree. The new fashion discovered by Marlowe was to abstract a single passion or humor and to envelop a character by it alone. This is a kind of vertical procedure which can be observed in Montaigne's painting of thought (*peinture de la pensée*), in which his self-portraiture invests him with his books, or in Breughel's and Poussin's sudden placing of figures in a landscape and not in front of it. The landscape could then function pictorially as humor or ruling passion in narrative, drama, or essay. In music this is called the discovery of harmony, and it succeeded the contrapuntal stacking of parallel themes one above the other in the style of the double plots of the popular drama.

It was Flaubert who abandoned the harmonic concentration on individual character as humor and who rediscovered the character as theme. By 1900 all of the arts had begun to use the same method again. But for our purposes it is only necessary to point to the replacing of contrapuntal by harmonic, vertical structure in music and the other arts as dependent on the new printed scores. For this new mode developed steadily until the idea of experiencing characters as created and defined by their natural settings became the norm. But first with Dickens, then Flaubert, then James Joyce in *Ulysses*, the city becomes not background but principal character or actor itself. Perhaps these brief notes on a very complex subject will serve to show how deep a shaft the printed word sank into the regions of human sensibility, perception, and expression. From an entirely different direction William Cobbett's A *Year's Residence in America* (1795) [20] can help us to get our bearings. In contrasting the English and Americans of 1795 Cobbett is talking of an England long before the bill of 1870 made literacy compulsory. He was amazed by an America in which literacy had long been voluntary.

Here is an excerpt from among many observations of the same theme:

> There are very few really ignorant men in America of native growth. Every farmer is more or less of a *reader*. There is no brogue, no *provincial dialect*. No class like that which the French call *peasantry* . . . they are all well-informed; modest without shyness; always free to communicate what they know, and never ashamed to acknowledge they have yet to learn. You never hear them *boast* of their possessions, and you never hear them *complaining* of their wants. They have all been readers from their youth up; and there are few subjects on which they cannot converse with you whether of a political or a scientific nature. At any rate they always *hear* with patience. I do not know that I ever heard a native

20 Chapman and Dodd, London, n.d., p. 157

> American interrupt another man while he was speaking. Their *sedateness* and *coolness*, the *deliberate* manner in which they say and do everything, and the *slowness* and *reserve* with which they express their assent; these are very wrongly estimated when they are taken for marks of a *want of feeling*. It must be a tale of woe indeed, that will bring a tear from an American's eye; but any trumped-up story will send his hand to his pocket . . . However, you will not, for a long while, know what to do for want of the *quick responses* of the English tongue, and the decided tone of the English expression. The *loud voice* and *hard squeeze* by the hand; the *instant assent* or dissent; the clamorous joy, the *bitter wailing*; the ardent friendship; the deadly enmity; the love that makes people kill themselves; the hatred that makes them kill others. All these belong to the characters of Englishmen, in whose minds and hearts every feeling exists in the *extreme*.

Today we would be unwilling to attribute any of these English characteristics to Englishmen. But we might be inclined to associate the American character of 1795 with the English of today. Highly literate English people have long ago sloughed off the vigorous other-directed manner of the Englishman, model 1795. The inner-directed man of David Riesman's [21] choice is the man of print culture, and Cobbett sketches him with gusto.

The *Essays* of Francis Bacon are a high instance of all the new characteristics of the reading and writing disciplines which were having such exciting results in 1600. Bacon's scientific program was frankly based on the printed book as offering a supreme instrument of applied science. For centuries men had spoken of the 'book of nature' meaning pages for contemplation and meditation. Bacon understood the resources of print technology very well. His idea was to catalogue the entire face of nature in systematic book form in such a way that as by a kind of synoptical device

---

21 *The Lonely Crowd*, Doubleday: Garden City, New York, 1953, p. 110ff

one could consult any phenomenon in a printed form. If the cataloguing were completely done in tables and columns, Bacon was sure that a child could read off the most profound natural laws which had been hidden from man since the fall of Adam. Bacon had no concern with speculative science. He wanted practical results for '*the relief of man's fallen estate.*' He was not mistaken in the power of print to provide the means of applied science. The methods of spelled-out and segmented processes have been at the base of all Western achievement. Technology is explicitness.

The inductive method is as hard to pin down as the literal interpretation of Scripture, but it would seem to be nothing less than the analytic habit of the literate mind in breaking up movement into static and manipulable segments. A great new turn was given this process by the Cartesian formula that we can discover causes by anticipating them with effects. In other words, we can initiate creative insight or, alternatively, we can retrace the creative process itself by working backwards from effects to causes. We can discover the unknown by tracking backwards from the known, in the manner of Poe and Doyle. Induction in this pattern enters the sphere of total reconstruction of actions and situations which is at one and the same time literary and scientific. And this simultaneous fusion of the analytic and the empathic has become the mark of the highest achievements of the past century in the arts and sciences alike. These methods and achievements are inseparable from the literary disciplines that are correlative with print.

The question remains whether our age has entered upon post-literacy via the electronic media and technology in a fashion which questions the entire validity of print and literacy. Print is analytic, visual, lineal, consecutive. The electronic is instant, auditory, and nuclear. We have lived with the electronic for over a century in the form of the telegraphic newspaper. Perhaps we can derive a clue from this newspaper about the shape of what is already here, remembering that during five centuries many subliminal motivations resulted from print technology but very little conscious grasp. The Soviet press today is still pre-telegraphic in form, by choice, of course. That is, all news is processed from a single literary viewpoint as in *Time* magazine. But *Time* is not a newspaper. It is a weekly digest of the news. With the telegraph, information began to flow at a different rate and in different patterns. Both speed and quantity imposed new styles of writing and editing. The news report had to be in the neutral style of 'objective' reporting if only because many items from many quarters had to appear, side by side. For the same reasons, the personal point of view in editorializing became precarious and even irrelevant. At electronic speed the newspaper page became a kind of global snapshot, day by day, long before the advent of the wirephoto. Moreover, the very small amount of processing of the huge quantity of information which was feasible after the telegraph really caused this job to pass from the editor to the reader. Western newspapers, that is to say, have for decades been a do-it-yourself package. And it is precisely the absence of explicit, editorialized news structure, as in *Time* magazine or the *London* and *New York Times*, that is taken as a mark of inferiority in the popular press. Yet it is the literary, carefully written papers that offer most of the pre-digested, processed and lineally inter-related news and views. This fact is overlooked because this kind of newspaper has so many strong affinities with literary culture that much is forgiven it.

If one studies the character of auditory space, the space preferred in oral culture, the central fact that emerges is that an auditory space is a spherical field of simultaneous relations. Such a field of relations is precisely what comes into existence by means of the telegraphic press. Space and time are reduced to the point where the globe as *seen* on the page becomes a simultaneous field of relations. That is to say, the press has become *essentially* auditory even while remaining a visual experience. This is the kind of reversal which overtook the manuscript with the advent of print. By retaining the form of the manuscript the printers were, none the less, able to provide readers with totally new experiences, which have been the theme of this chapter.

I suggest that the real reversal which has overtaken print technology is to be found in the photograph and the movie, and that these forms of total 'statement without syntax,' as William Ivins describes it, are utterly unlike telegraph, radio, and TV. Somehow we must unriddle the complex of new messages involved in this new situation which has been created by print technology itself. So far nothing has been done to explicate the situation because we still imagine that these forms of codifying information can co-exist without transforming one another. This attitude, now suicidal, is yet a natural legacy of print culture. Is it not, therefore, an obligation of the beneficiaries of that great culture to organize some research into the new situation? Psychologists, if asked, are quite capable of explicating the psychodynamics of perception resulting from print in its relation to the new electronic media. At present a stalemate has occurred with the teachers of language and literature lining up against the electronic threat. In the new time which must be one of co-existence and pluralism there will be a basis for the simultaneous use of print and of all other media as well. To discover that basis now before we exhaust ourselves in moral denunciation and pointless clashes is urgently indicated.

In his Aquinas lecture for 1958, the physicist Henry Margenau [22] announced a basic change which has come over the intellectual world:

> Many of us, especially the scholars in the liberal arts and nearly all newspaper men, still look upon science as a catalogue of dead but certified facts. Our teaching largely reflects this view. A first course in physics, chemistry, or biology has come to be identified with a certain subject, a collection of facts sometimes unilluminated by ideas, hanging together as a traditional aggregate and forming a whole which is exactly the sum of the parts. When told that a student has had half a course in elementary physics one knows accurately what this means. And one also knows that the course contained no ideas, for ideas in contradistinction to facts do not obey the laws of arithmetic. Laws are presented as inductive generalizations of observational experience, never as bold conjectures, as ideas defying the knowledge of their day, which is, indeed, the status wherein most of them were born.

Professor Margenau here proclaims the visionary quality of scientific discovery and suggests that our print culture now exerts an unfavorable effect in our curricula. Because print favors the catalogue, the definite and the precise rather than adventuresome exploration, here is a suitable challenge to the world of printers and readers to meet the demands of a new age with new discovery and resources of their medium.

---

22 *Thomas and the Physics of 1858: A Confrontation*, Marquette University Press, Milwaukee, 1958, p. 45

Printing and Social Change
Marshall McLuhan - Unbound (01)

ISBN: 1-58423-051-7
Library of Congress Control Number 2005927213

Marshall McLuhan Unbound Project Editors
Eric McLuhan, W. Terrence Gordon

Published in United States in October 2005 by
Gingko Press, Inc.
5768 Paradise Drive, Suite J • Corte Madera, CA 94925
(415) 924-9615 • Fax (415) 924-9608
email: books@gingkopress.com
http://www.gingkopress.com

Design, packaging and production: Die Gestalten Verlag, Berlin
Layout and Typography: onlab, Berlin
Fonts: *Dolly* by Underware, *Bullet* by House Industries
Production: Martin Bretschneider, Vinzenz Geppert
Art direction: Robert Klanten

Made in Germany

embodied in critical articles and reviews. For information address Gingko Press.